D0466634

To:

From:

Live Love Laugh

Compiled by Evelyn Beilenson

Illustrated by Donna Ingemanson

PETER PAUPER PRESS, INC.
White Plains, New York

Illustrations copyright © 2008
Donna Ingemanson

Designed by Heather Zschock

Copyright © 2008
Peter Pauper Press, Inc.
202 Mamaroneck Avenue
White Plains, NY 10601
All rights reserved
ISBN 978-1-59359-896-9
Printed in China
7 6 5 4

Visit us at www.peterpauper.com

Introduction

It's not easy to *live* well, *love* passionately, and *laugh* with abandon. It often requires taking risks. As Dorothy Thompson said, "Only when we are no longer afraid do we begin to *live*." Living well means also daring to *love* without restraint, summed up famously by Tennyson, when he wrote, "'Tis better

to have loved and lost than never to have loved at all." And for heaven's sake, don't forget to *laugh*. Laughter is the only tranquilizer with no side effects. So go out there and take a chance. **Live** well, *laugh* often, and *love* much. Make yourself and the world around you a happier and richer place.

—E. B.

Live your life and
forget your age.

—NORMAN VINCENT PEALE

The best things in life
aren't things.

—ART BUCHWALD

And in the end,
it's not the years in
your life that count.
It's the life in
your years.

—ABRAHAM LINCOLN

Let us so live that when we come to die even the undertaker will be sorry.

—MARK TWAIN

You don't get to choose how
you're going to die. Or when.
You can only decide how
you're going to live. Now.

—JOAN BAEZ

Everything has
been figured out,
except how to live.

—Jean-Paul Sartre

Life is what happens
while you're busy
making other plans.

—JOHN LENNON

Life can only be
understood backwards,
but it must be lived
forward.

—SØREN KIERKEGAARD

You can't do anything about the length of your life, but you can do something about its width and depth.

—Evan Esar

There is no cure for birth and death, save to enjoy the interval.

—George Santayana

So live that you
wouldn't be ashamed to
sell the family parrot
to the town gossip.

—WILL ROGERS

Learn from
yesterday, live for
today, hope for
tomorrow.

—AUTHOR UNKNOWN

Only a life lived
for others is a life
worthwhile.

—ALBERT EINSTEIN

If you are not too long, I will wait here for you all my life.

—OSCAR WILDE

Only when we are no
longer afraid do we
begin to live.

—DOROTHY THOMPSON

Life would be infinitely happier
if we could only be born at the
age of eighty and gradually
approach eighteen.

—MARK TWAIN

It is only possible to live happily ever after on a day to day basis.

—MARGARET BONNANO

May you live all the
days of your life.

—Jonathan Swift

I could not, at any age,
be content to take my place by
the fireside and simply look on.
Life was meant to be lived.
Curiosity must be kept alive.
One must never, for whatever
reason, turn his back on life.

—ELEANOR ROOSEVELT

Keep breathing.

—Sophie Tucker

Where there is love
there is life.

—MOHANDAS K. GANDHI

There is time for work.
And time for love.
That leaves no other time.

—Coco Chanel

There is only one
happiness in life—
to love and to be loved.

~George Sand

Each moment of a happy
lover's hour is worth an age
of dull and common life.

—APHRA BEHN

I hold it true, whate'er befall;
I feel it, when I sorrow most;
'Tis better to have loved and lost
Than never to have loved at all.

—ALFRED, LORD TENNYSON

Life is the flower
for which love
is the honey.

—VICTOR HUGO

Infantile love follows
the principle:
"I love because I am loved."
Mature love follows
the principle:
"I am loved because I love."
Immature love says:
"I love you because I need you."
Mature love says:
"I need you because I love you."

—ERICH FROMM

Love doesn't make
the world go 'round;
love is what makes
the ride worthwhile.

—FRANKLIN P. JONES

Love sought is good,
but given unsought
is better.

—SHAKESPEARE

The Eskimos have 52 words for snow because it is so special to them; there ought to be as many for love!

—MARGARET ATWOOD

Who so loves believes
the impossible.

—ELIZABETH BARRETT BROWNING

When we can't have
what we love we must
love what we have.

—Roger de Bussy-Rabutin

Love is like war:
easy to begin but very
hard to stop.

—H. L. MENCKEN

In expressing love we belong among the undeveloped countries.

—SAUL BELLOW

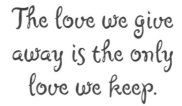

The love we give
away is the only
love we keep.

—ELBERT HUBBARD

One should always be wary of someone who promises their love will last longer than a weekend.

—QUENTIN CRISP

That Love is all
there is
Is all we know
of Love.

—Emily Dickinson

Do you want me to tell you something really subversive? Love is everything it's cracked up to be. That's why people are so cynical about it. It really is worth fighting for, being brave for, risking everything for. And the trouble is, if you don't risk anything, you risk even more.

—ERICA JONG

Love: A temporary
insanity curable
by marriage.

—AMBROSE BIERCE

There is no remedy
for love but to
love more.

—HENRY DAVID THOREAU

Age does not protect
you from love,
but love to some extent
protects you from age.

—JEANNE MOREAU

Love cures people—
both the ones who give it
and the ones who receive it.

–KARL A. MENNINGER

Love is blind,
but marriage
restores its sight.

—George Lichtenberg

If love is the answer,
could you rephrase
the question?

—LILY TOMLIN

Love is the only force
capable of transforming
an enemy into a friend.

—Martin Luther King, Jr.

The hunger for love
is much more difficult
to remove than the
hunger for bread.

—MOTHER TERESA

Laughter is the only tranquilizer with no side effects.

—AUTHOR UNKNOWN

Successful people live well, laugh often, and love much. They've filled a niche and accomplished tasks so as to leave the world better than they found it, while looking for the best in others, and giving the best they have.

—RALPH WALDO EMERSON

A man isn't
poor if he can
still laugh.

—RAYMOND HITCHCOCK

Laughter is the
shortest distance
between two people.

—Victor Borge

Nobody ever died
of laughter.

—Sir Max Beerbohm

You grow up on the day you have your first real laugh at yourself.

—ETHEL BARRYMORE

Laughter is the closest thing to the grace of God.

—KARL BARTH

What soap is to
the body, laughter
is to the soul.

—YIDDISH PROVERB

Laugh and the world laughs with you; snore and you sleep alone.

—ANTHONY BURGESS

Laughter is an instant vacation.

—MILTON BERLE

We are all here for a
spell; get all the good
laughs you can.

—WILL ROGERS

Always laugh
when you can.
It is cheap medicine.

—LORD BYRON

He who laughs
has not yet heard
the bad news.

—BERTOLT BRECHT

I've always thought that a big laugh is a really loud noise from the soul saying, "Ain't that the truth."

—QUINCY JONES

Life does not cease to be funny

when people die any more than it

ceases to be serious when people laugh.

~George Bernard Shaw

The best way to make your audience laugh is to start laughing yourself.

—OLIVER GOLDSMITH

Mirth is God's medicine.
Everybody ought
to bathe in it.

—HENRY WARD BEECHER

Man, when you lose
your laugh you lose
your footing.

—KEN KESEY

Laughter is the
language of the soul.

—PABLO NERUDA